# Dinosaurs Alive!

# Triceratops

## and other horned and armoured dinosaurs

Jinny Johnson

Illustrated by Graham Rosewarne

FRANKLIN WATTS
LONDON•SYDNEY

An Appleseed Editions book

First published in 2007 by Franklin Watts

Franklin Watts
338 Euston Road, London NW1 3BH

Franklin Watts Australia
Hachette Children's Books
Level 17/207 Kent St, Sydney, NSW 2000

© 2007 Appleseed Editions

Created by Appleseed Editions Ltd,
Well House, Friars Hill, Guestling,
East Sussex TN35 4ET

Designed by Helen James
Edited by Mary-Jane Wilkins
Artwork by Graham Rosewarne

ISBN  978 07496 7541 7

Dewey Classification: 567.915' 8

A CIP catalogue for this book is available from the British Library

Printed in China

Franklin Watts is a division of Hachette Children's Books

# Contents

# Dinosaurs' world

A dinosaur was a kind of reptile that lived millions of years ago. Dinosaurs lived long before there were people on Earth.

We know about dinosaurs because many of their bones and teeth have been discovered. Scientists called palaeontologists (pay-lee-on-tol-ojists) learn a lot about the animals by studying these bones.

The first dinosaurs lived about 225 million years ago. They disappeared – became extinct – about 65 million years ago.

Some scientists believe that birds are a type of dinosaur so they say there are still dinosaurs living all around us!

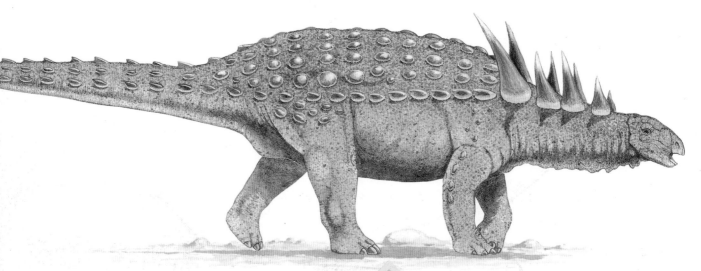

*Sauropelta*

# TRIASSIC
**248 to 205 million years ago**
Some dinosaurs that lived at this time:
Coelophysis, Eoraptor, Liliensternus, Plateosaurus,
Riojasaurus, Saltopus

# EARLY JURASSIC
**205 to 180 million years ago**
Some dinosaurs that lived at this time:
Crylophosaurus, Dilophosaurus, Lesothosaurus,
Massospondylus, Scelidosaurus, Scutellosaurus

# LATE JURASSIC
**180 to 144 million years ago**
Some dinosaurs that lived at this time:
Allosaurus, Apatosaurus, Brachiosaurus,
Ornitholestes, Stegosaurus, Yangchuanosaurus

*Stegosaurus*

# EARLY CRETACEOUS
**144 to 98 million years ago**
Some dinosaurs that lived at this time:
Baryonyx, Giganotosaurus, Iguanodon, Leaellynasaura,
Muttaburrasaurus, Nodosaurus, Sauropelta

# LATE CRETACEOUS
**98 to 65 million years ago**
Some dinosaurs that lived at this time:
Ankylosaurus, Gallimimus, Maiasaura, Triceratops,
Tyrannosaurus, Velociraptor

*Tyrannosaurus*

# Triceratops

Imagine a huge creature, twice the size of
a rhinoceros, with an enormous horned head.

*A full-grown Triceratops
weighed up to ten
tonnes – as much
as two elephants.*

Triceratops had three sharp horns
and a large bony frill at the back
of its neck. The name Triceratops
means three-horned face.

This dinosaur lived in North
America. It was one of the biggest
of all the horned dinosaurs.

*Dinosaurs lived long before
there were people on Earth.
But here you can see how
big a dinosaur was compared
with a seven-year-old child.*

6

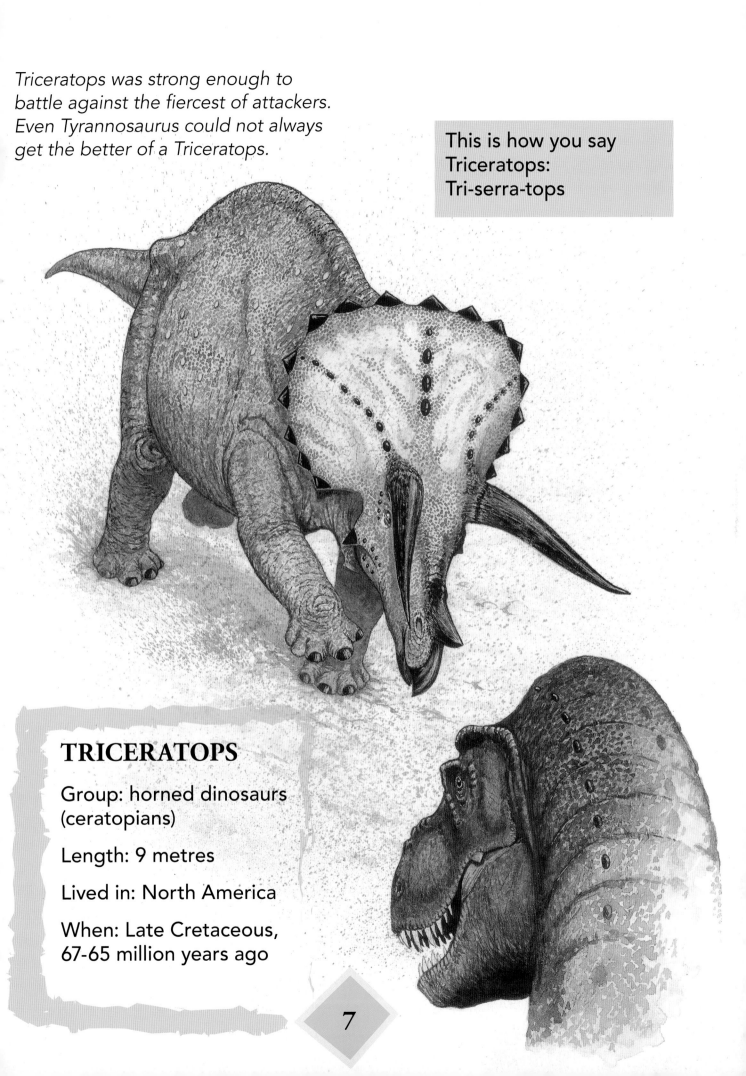

*Triceratops was strong enough to battle against the fiercest of attackers. Even Tyrannosaurus could not always get the better of a Triceratops.*

This is how you say Triceratops:
Tri-serra-tops

## TRICERATOPS

Group: horned dinosaurs
(ceratopians)

Length: 9 metres

Lived in: North America

When: Late Cretaceous,
67-65 million years ago

# Inside Triceratops

The head of Triceratops measured as much as two metres from the tip of the nose to the back of its head – more than the length of an adult human. That is a very big head!

Triceratops had two long horns on its forehead – each a metre long. Even the little horn on its nose was 18 centimetres long.

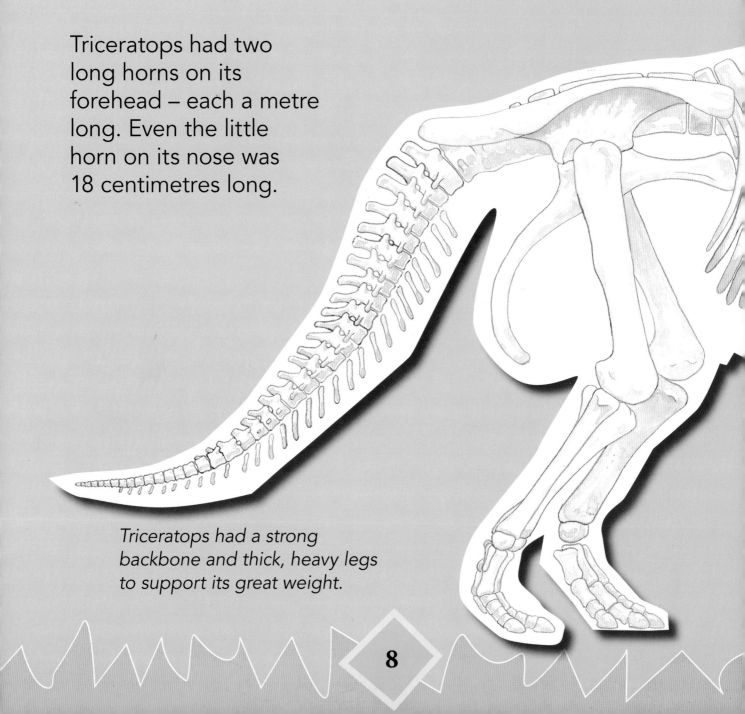

*Triceratops had a strong backbone and thick, heavy legs to support its great weight.*

The enormous frill at the back of this dinosaur's head was made of solid bone. It was very heavy and strong, so other creatures found it difficult to attack Triceratops.

*Look at this dinosaur's jaws. It has a beak like a parrot's. This strong, sharp beak helped the dinosaur chop off mouthfuls of tough plants.*

# Triceratops in action

Triceratops lived in large groups called herds.
Together the animals wandered slowly through
the forests, feeding on plants.

Triceratops may look fierce, but
it preferred to stay out of trouble.
Few other dinosaurs dared to attack
such a large, well-armoured animal.

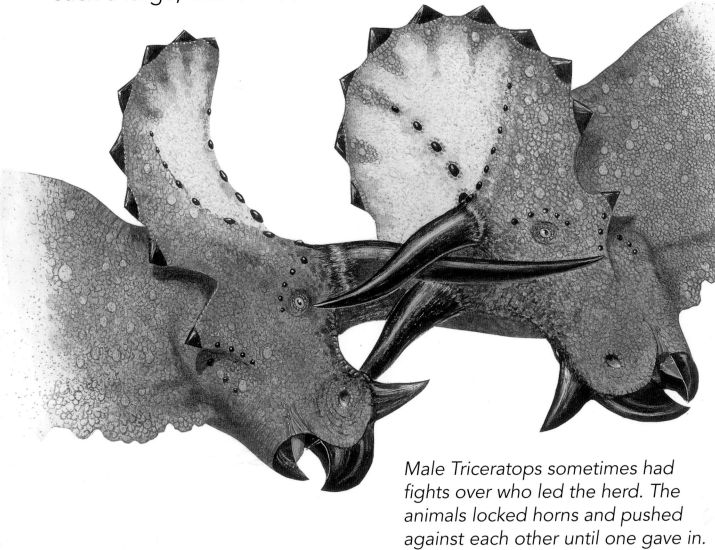

*Male Triceratops sometimes had
fights over who led the herd. The
animals locked horns and pushed
against each other until one gave in.*

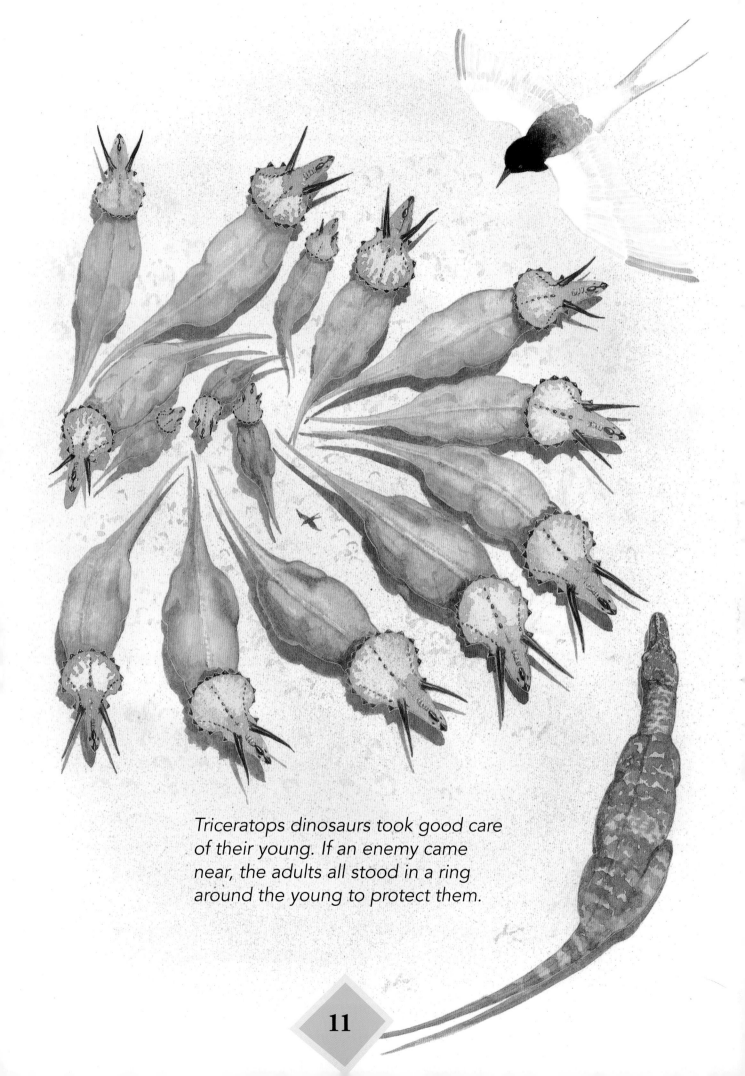

Triceratops dinosaurs took good care of their young. If an enemy came near, the adults all stood in a ring around the young to protect them.

# Short-frilled dinosaurs

There were other kinds of horned dinosaur, as well as Triceratops. Some had short neck frills. Others had longer ones.

Centrosaurus was a short-frilled dinosaur and smaller than Triceratops. The long horn on its nose and the spikes on its neck frill made it look very ferocious. Centrosaurus lived in herds and fed on plants.

This is how you say
Centrosaurus:
Cen-tro-sore-us

# CENTROSAURUS

Group: horned dinosaurs (ceratopians)

Length: 6 metres

Lived in: North America

When: Late Cretaceous, 76-74 million years ago

# PACHYRHINOSAURUS

Group: horned dinosaurs (ceratopians)

Length: 6 metres

Lived in: North America

When: Late Cretaceous, 76-74 million years ago

*Pachyrhinosaurus may not have had horns. The skulls have just a thick bony pad on the nose. But the horns might have fallen off and got lost!*

This is how you say Pachyrhinosaurus: Pack-ee-rine-o-sore-us

# Long-frilled dinosaurs

Another group of horned dinosaurs had very long neck frills. Torosaurus was one of these. It had the largest skull of any land animal ever known.

The dinosaur's head and huge neck frill measured more than 2.5 metres. Its horns and frill made it very hard to attack.

*Some experts think that Torosaurus's neck frill may have been covered with colourful skin.*

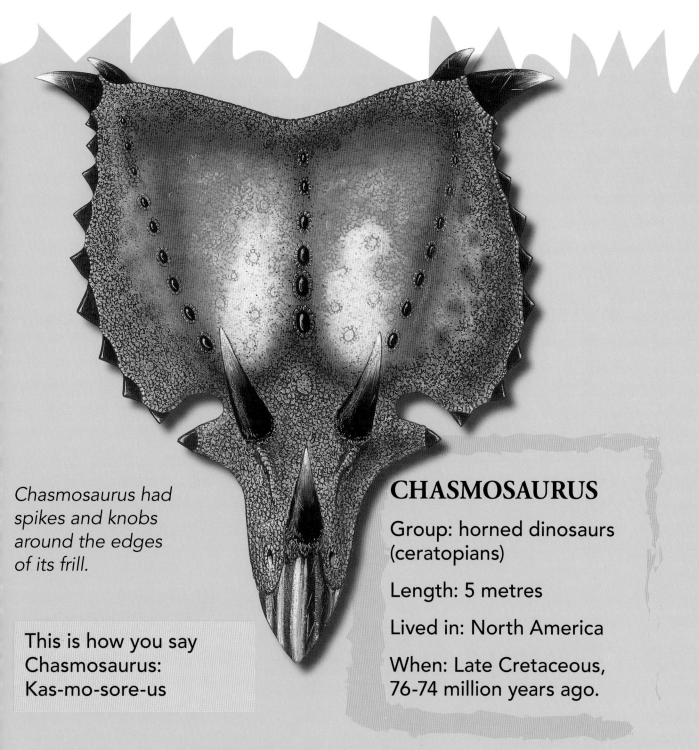

*Chasmosaurus had spikes and knobs around the edges of its frill.*

This is how you say Chasmosaurus: Kas-mo-sore-us

## CHASMOSAURUS

Group: horned dinosaurs (ceratopians)

Length: 5 metres

Lived in: North America

When: Late Cretaceous, 76-74 million years ago.

## TOROSAURUS

Group: horned dinosaurs (ceratopians)

Length: 7.5 metres

Lived in: North America

When: Late Cretaceous, 70-65 million years ago

This is how you say Torosaurus: Tor-o-sore-us

# Armoured dinosaurs: nodosaurs

Armoured dinosaurs had built-in suits of armour – flat pieces of bone, set into their skin. Many also had spikes sticking out at the sides of the body.

There were two groups of armoured dinosaurs – nodosaurs and ankylosaurs. Nodosaurs were huge, tank-like creatures. Two of the largest were Sauropelta and Panoplosaurus.

This is how you say Sauropelta:
Sore-o-pelt-ah

*Sauropelta was the biggest nodosaur and was heavier than a rhinoceros.*

16

# PANOPLOSAURUS

Group: armoured dinosaurs (nodosaurs)

Length: 7 metres

Lived in: North America

When: Late Cretaceous, 79-75 million years ago

This is how you say Panoplosaurus:
Pan-o-ploh-sore-us

*Panoplosaurus even had plates of bone on its head as extra protection.*

# SAUROPELTA

Group: armoured dinosaurs (nodosaurs)

Length: 6.5 metres

Lived in: North America

When: Early Cretaceous, 121-94 million years ago

# Armoured dinosaurs: ankylosaurs

Ankylosaurs were even more heavily armoured than nodosaurs. They had a tail with a heavy club of bone at its tip to swing against an attacker. Even their eyelids had pieces of bone that came down over them like shutters.

*Saichania, like all ankylosaurs, ate plants. It could chop big mouthfuls with the sharp beak at the front of its mouth.*

This is how you say
Saichania:
Sy-chan-ee-a

## SAICHANIA

Group: armoured dinosaurs
(ankylosaurs)

Length: 6.5 metres

Lived in: Mongolia

When: Late Cretaceous,
80 million years ago

# EUOPLOCEPHALUS

Group: armoured dinosaurs (ankylosaurs)

Length: 7 metres

Lived in: North America

When: Late Cretaceous, 76-70 million years ago

*If attacked, Euoplocephalus used all its strength to hit its enemy with its clubbed tail. This heavy ball of bone could break another animal's legs.*

This is how you say Euoplocephalus:
You-o-plo-kef-a-lus

# Boneheaded dinosaurs

These dinosaurs had amazing dome-shaped skulls made of a thick lump of bone – like a built-in helmet.

Male boneheaded dinosaurs probably fought fierce battles in the breeding season – just as goats do today. Their bony heads would have protected them as they crashed into one another.

This is how you say Stegoceras:
Steg-os-er-as

## STEGOCERAS

Group: boneheaded dinosaurs

Length: 2.4 metres

Lived in: North America

When: Late Cretaceous, 76-74 million years ago

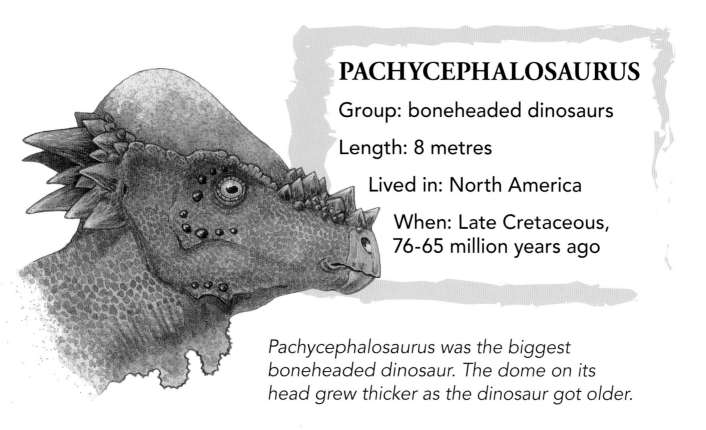

# PACHYCEPHALOSAURUS

Group: boneheaded dinosaurs

Length: 8 metres

Lived in: North America

When: Late Cretaceous, 76-65 million years ago

*Pachycephalosaurus was the biggest boneheaded dinosaur. The dome on its head grew thicker as the dinosaur got older.*

*Male Stegoceras dinosaurs fought by charging towards each other and clashing head on. They held their tails out behind to balance.*

This is how you say Pachycephalosaurus: Pack-ee-kef-al-o-sore-us

**21**

# Stegosaurs

These dinosaurs are very easy to recognize. They all have large, triangular-shaped bony plates along their back.

Stegosaurus was the biggest of the stegosaurs. Although its body was huge (bigger than an elephant's) it had a tiny head, which was only 40 centimetres long.

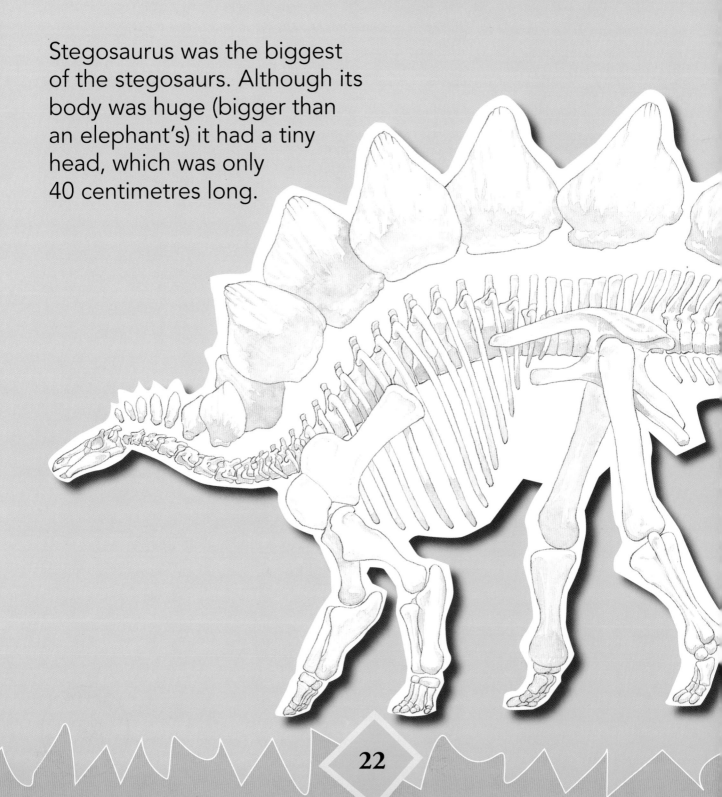

Stegosaurus's big back legs were much longer than its front legs. This made the dinosaur's body slope forward so its mouth was nearer the ground when it was feeding.

## STEGOSAURUS

Group: stegosaurs

Length: 9 metres

Found in: North America

When: Late Jurassic, 155-144 million years ago

This is how you say Stegosaurus: Steg-oh-sore-us.

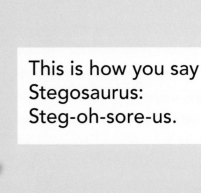

*Stegosaurus had big, heavy leg bones and a strong backbone to support its great weight. It used the long spikes at the end of its tail to defend itself.*

# Spiky stegosaurs

Stegosaurus had two rows of large bony plates running from its neck to its tail. The biggest was 60 centimetres high.

Scientists aren't sure why stegosaurs had plates, but many think they helped the animals warm up or cool down, and made them more difficult to attack.

*Lexovisaurus had a sharp spike on each shoulder.*

## LEXOVISAURUS

Group: stegosaurs

Length: 5-6 metres

Lived in: Europe (England and France)

When: Late Jurassic, 170-150 million years ago

This is how you say Lexovisaurus:
Lex-o-vee-sore-us

When the stegosaur was cold it turned towards the sun. The heat of the sun warmed the blood as it passed through the skin on the plates. When the dinosaur felt too hot it faced the wind, which cooled the plates and the dinosaur's blood.

This is how you say Tuojiangosaurus:
Too-yang-o-sore-us

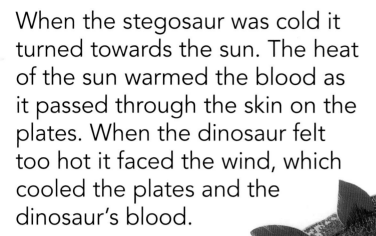

*Tuojiangosaurus defended itself with its long spiky tail.*

## TUOJIANGOSAURUS

Group: stegosaurs

Length: 7 metres

Lived in: China

When: Late Jurassic, 157-154 million years ago

# Stegosaurus in action

Stegosaurus gobbled up tough leaves
with the sharp, toothless beak at
the front of its mouth.

The dinosaur had small teeth at the
back of its jaws to grind down the
leaves. It moved around on four
legs, but could probably rear up on
its back legs to reach high leaves.

*Stegosaurus
probably spent
most of the day
feeding, just
as plant-eating
animals do today.*

Stegosaurus was not a fast runner. If danger threatened, it could lash out at an attacker with its heavy, spiked tail.

# Dinosaur plants

Triceratops and other horned and armoured dinosaurs all fed on plants. These big creatures needed a huge amount of food every day – what kind of plants did they eat?

When the first dinosaurs lived, during the Triassic, plants looked very different from the ones we see today. There were no flowering plants and no grass. The Earth was much drier than it is now, but there were plants such as conifer trees, ferns, horsetails and palm-like cycads (sy-kads).

cycad

fern

horsetails

During the Jurassic period the weather became wetter and cooler. More and more types of conifers grew and ferns became as tall as trees.

*conifer*

*tree fern*

## FLOWERING PLANTS

The first plants with flowers and fruits appeared in Cretaceous times. There was more food for plant-eating dinosaurs than ever before and great herds roamed the forests. More and more flowering plants grew, and some earlier plants, such as cycads, became rare.

*sycamore*

*magnolia*

# Words to remember

**armoured dinosaurs**
Dinosaurs covered with bony spikes and plates to help protect them from enemies. There were two types of armoured dinosaurs – ankylosaurs and nodosaurs.

**boneheaded dinosaurs**
Dinosaurs with a large bony bump on the skull. It protected the dinosaur's head in head-butting battles between rivals in the breeding season. Stegoceras was a boneheaded dinosaur.

**carnivore**
An animal that eats other animals. Tyrannosaurus was a carnivore.

**conifer**
A type of tree with leaves like little needles. Yews, pines and monkey puzzle trees are all conifers.

**cycads**
Palm-like trees that grew in the days of the dinosaurs. Some cycads still grow today in hot parts of the world.

**fossil**
Parts of an animal such as bones and teeth that have been preserved in rock over millions of years.

**herbivore**
An animal that eats plants. Triceratops was a herbivore.

## horned dinosaurs

Dinosaurs with big pointed horns and a sheet of bone called a frill at the back of the head. Triceratops was a horned dinosaur.

## neck frill

The sheet of bone at the back of a horned dinosaur's head.

## palaeontologist

A scientist who looks for and studies fossils to find out more about the creatures of the past.

## reptile

An animal with a backbone and a dry scaly body. Most reptiles lay eggs. Dinosaurs were reptiles. Today's reptiles include lizards, snakes and crocodiles.

## tyrannosaur

A type of large meat-eating dinosaur such as Tyrannosaurus which attacked plant-eating dinosaurs.

# Index